CISCO

NETWORKS

FOR

BEGINNERS

Learn The Basics in One Day

By

Dr Issa Ngoie

Introduction

<u>Cisco</u> is a US technology company that is best known for its networking products.

Headquartered in California – its name is short for San Francisco – it develops, manufactures and sells networking <u>hardware</u>, <u>telecoms</u> equipment and other IT services and products.

The company was founded in **1984 by Leonard Bosack** and **Sandy Lerner**. The pair pioneered the concept of the Local Area Network (LAN) being used to connect computers over large distances using a multiprotocol router system.

This put Cisco in a good position to capitalise on the rise of the <u>World Wide Web</u> in the 1990s, with the company outlasting many competitors who failed during the dot-com bubble.

What does Cisco do?

Cisco has a massive roster of <u>products and services</u>, including:

- **Networking**: Cisco provides products and services to help companies build computer networks, including switches, routers and software at individual, small business and industrial scales.
- **Wireless and Mobility**: The company creates solutions for wireless communications, including access points, wireless controllers and network management
- **Security**: network security products include <u>DDoS</u> protection, firewalls and <u>multi-factor authentication</u>
- **Collaboration**: the firm helps to facilitate companies and employees to to collaborate, including through <u>working from home</u> and remote administration

- **Data Centres**: *Cisco helps clients to create <u>cloud computing</u> networks and manage their infrastructure*

Contents

Cisco stock and valuation

When **Cisco** went public in 1990 on the NASDAQ, the company's market cap totalled $224 million. Cisco then earned the moniker of the most valuable company in the world by 2000 with a more than $500 billion market cap.

As of July 2022, the company had 83,300 employees worldwide. However, it has announced plans to restructure and cut as many as 5% of staff.

Cisco's reported $51.6 billion annual revenue in Q4 of the 2022 financial year. Its share price has been fluctuating between $46 and $50 in the first two months of 2022.

Certifications: Build Your IT Future

Cisco career certifications bring valuable, measurable rewards to technology professionals and to the organizations that employ them.

Explore career certification paths below that meet your professional development goals.

Entry	Associate	Professional	Expert
Starting point for individuals interested in starting a career as a networking professional	Master the essentials needed to launch a rewarding career and expand your job possibilities with the latest technologies.	Select core technology track and a focused concentration exam to customize your professional-level certification	This certification is accepted worldwide as the most prestigious certification in the technology industry.
Cisco Certified Support Technician (CCST)	CCNA	CCNP Enterprise	CCIE Enterprise Infrastructure
			CCIE Enterprise Wireless
		CCNP Collaboration	CCIE Collaboration
		CCNP Data Center	CCIE Data Center
		CCNP Security	CCIE Security
		CCNP Service Provider	CCIE Service Provider
			CCDE
	CyberOps Associate	CyberOps Professional	
	DevNet Associate	DevNet Professional	DevNet Expert

Besides the leading networking giant, Cisco technology and **Cisco hardware** influence the whole networking world, for it is always supplying the advanced networking solutions and perfect **Cisco network equipment**. Cisco certification, wide range of products, scalability, manageability, reliability, enterprise class features, cost, all these factors make you no hesitate to choose Cisco.

Today's businesses require a network platform that enables technology innovation and business-critical services across the entire network. Cisco stands alone in its ability to provide an end-to-end network platform tied together by a common infrastructure and a common operating system, and manageable as a single, cohesive entity.

Only **Cisco** can provide the platform for campus, branch, data center, and wide-area networks that are highly available while integrating security at all levels of the network, helping to ensure the optimized delivery of application and communications, and providing inherent manageability. This platform includes:

Routing: Cisco offers the only routers that allow organizations to build a foundation for an intelligent, self-defending network, featuring best-in-class security services and routing technologies for the lowest total cost of ownership and highest return on investment.

Switching: Cisco offers one of the industry's most comprehensive portfolios of intelligent network switches, providing a continuously expanding suite of intelligent services and advanced technologies to strengthen, simplify, and extend the value of the network infrastructure.

Cisco IOS Software: Cisco IOS Software operates across routers and switches to enable an infrastructure that is highly available, secure, manageable, flexible, and scalable, and upon which businesses can quickly and confidently deploy advanced technologies.

Network Management: Cisco offers management tools and applications that ease network deployment, improve operational efficiency, increase network uptime, and reduce total cost of ownership.

Why Cisco Is the Best ....

- Customized ASICs allow better interoperability and support for an end-to-end solution with Cisco transceivers, routers, phones, and wireless access points.
- Single Cisco IOS Software train creates feature parity across all switching platforms versus

multiple outsourced software trains used by competitors.

- Ease-of-use applications and tools simplify network management while maintaining wire-speed performance:

  - ➤ Express setup
  - ➤ Smartports
  - ➤ Auto-QoS
  - ➤ DHCP autoconfiguration
  - ➤ Cisco Network Assistant

Become a Network Engineer

Behind every IT infrastructure is a Network Engineer. Network Engineers are experts who can apply a range of technologies to connect, secure, and automate complex networks, and it's a critical role in companies from every industry.

What does a Network Engineer do?

Design and build

Network Engineers design, build, and automate physical and wireless networks. Their goal is to ensure connectivity between phones, computers, routers, intranets, extranets, and more.

Optimize

Network Engineers look for ways to improve infrastructure. For example, they implement solutions to automate rote tasks, and work with vendors and colleagues to integrate new technologies into existing networks.

Monitor

Network Engineers observe and troubleshoot their systems to keep them running smoothly. They analyze network performance, test network functionality, and more.

What is a Network?

A **network** consists of two or more computers that are linked in order to share resources (such as printers and CDs), exchange files, or allow electronic communications. The computers on a network may be linked through cables, telephone lines, radio waves, satellites, or infrared light beams.

A NETWORK = GROUP OF OBJECTS

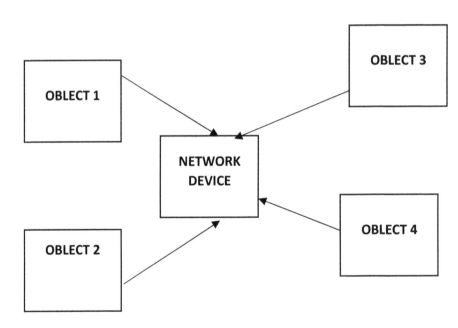

Example of objects

- ➤ Phones
- ➤ Tablets
- ➤ Printers
- ➤ Cameras
- ➤ Computers
- ➤ ......

Objects in a network are connected using :

- ➤ Cables
- ➤ Wirelless

Cisco

Types of network cables

Network cables can be divided into four types: coaxial, shielded twisted pair (STP), unshielded twisted pair (UTP), or fibre optic.

- ➢ *Coaxial Cables. ...*
- ➢ *Shielded Twisted Pair Cables. ...*
- ➢ *Unshielded Twisted Pair Cables. ...*
- ➢ *Fibre Optic Cables.*

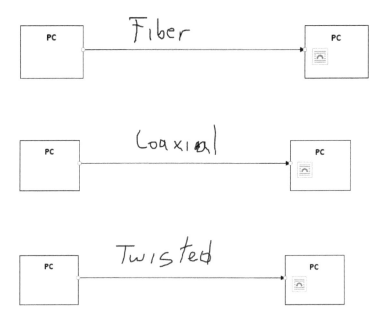

How to differentiate the types of network cables?

There are three primary types of **network cables** that are used in modern communication systems: fiber optic coaxial, and twisted pair. Each of them can be used for different purposes and is therefore unique. However, they have something in common, they all can perfectly work for **network communication**. So how is each one different in terms of specifications and features? What are the differences in performance and capacity between fiber optic cables, twisted pair cables, and coaxial cables?. We will analyze their main characteristics to find out.

Fiber Optic Cables

Fiber optic cables, also known as optical fiber cable, is a type of **Ethernet cable** that consists of one or several optic fibers used to transmit data. **Fiber optic cable** transmits data by sending light pulses through tiny tubes made of glass. These cables have a transmission capacity 26,000 times greater than twisted-pair cables.

These types of cables can be classified into single-mode fiber and multimode fibers. A single-mode optical fiber only allows one mode to propagate at once. It has a smaller core. In contrast, multimode fiber cables have a larger core that can simultaneously carry multiple light rays. The single-mode fiber cable can transmit for several kilometers, while multimode fiber is able to do it for up to 550m over a 10G network.

Twisted Pair Cable

Twisted pair cable is used frequently for telephone communications and modern **Ethernet Networks**. It is a type of wiring where two conductors in a single circuit are twisted., making a circuit that can transmit data. To protect against noise from adjacent pairs, the pairs are twisted together.

Coaxial Cable

<u>Coaxial cable</u> (or coax cable) is a popular choice for many applications; however, it is mainly used to transmit high-frequency signals. It is made up of a copper conductor with three layers of insulation and shielding that prevent crosstalk from motors, lighting, and other sources of EMI. The shield construction allows for longer **coaxial cables** between two devices.

There are many versions of this cable available, but only two — RG59 and RG6 — are most commonly used in residential applications. The name "RG" is a World War II term that means "radio guide", but it doesn't mean anything today.

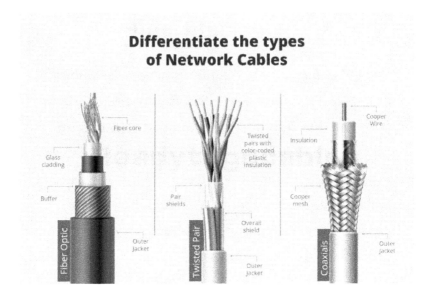

Differentiate the types of Network Cables

What is the difference?

These three types of cables, in some scenarios, have similar uses, but it is possible to differentiate them for their performance and capacity.

Coaxial cables and **twisted pair cables** are built using copper or copper-based wire and are surrounded by insulation with other materials. Both can transmit television, telephone, and data using electrical signals. Fiber optic cables, on the contrary, can send out the same signals at a higher frequency, with a wider bandwidth and faster speed. They are made from delicate, flexible tubes of plastic or glass.

Which one is cheaper?

Fiber optic cable is generally more expensive than copper because of its superior performance and capacity. However, prices for coaxial, twisted pair and fiber optic cables vary among vendors and suppliers in the cable market. It is crucial to compare these cables before you buy them.

Two very common types of networks include:

- ➢ Local Area Network (LAN)
- ➢ Wide Area Network (WAN)

Local Area Network

A **Local Area Network (LAN)** is a network that is confined to a relatively small area. It is generally limited to a geographic area such as a writing lab, school, or building.

Computers connected to a network are broadly categorized as servers or workstations. Servers are generally not used by humans directly, but rather run continuously to provide "services" to the other computers (and their human users) on the network. Services provided can include printing and faxing, software hosting, file storage and sharing, messaging, data storage and retrieval, complete access control (security) for the network's resources, and many others.

Workstations are called such because they typically do have a human user which interacts with the network through them. Workstations were traditionally considered a desktop, consisting of a computer, keyboard, display, and mouse, or a laptop, with with integrated keyboard, display, and touchpad. With the advent of the tablet computer, and the touch screen devices such as iPad and iPhone, our definition of workstation is quickly evolving to include those devices, because of their ability to interact with the network and utilize network services.

Servers tend to be more powerful than workstations, although configurations are guided by needs. For example, a group of servers might be located in a secure area, away from humans, and only accessed through the network. In such cases, it would be common for the servers to operate without a dedicated display or keyboard. However, the size and speed of the server's processor(s), hard drive, and main memory might add dramatically to the cost of the system. On the other hand, a workstation might not need as much storage or working memory, but might require an expensive display to accommodate the needs of its user.

Every computer on a network should be appropriately configured for its use.

On a single LAN, computers and servers may be connected by cables or wirelessly. Wireless access to a wired network is made possible by wireless access points (WAPs). These WAP devices provide a bridge between computers and networks. A typical WAP might have the theoretical capacity to connect hundreds or even thousands of wireless users to a network, although practical capacity might be far less.

Nearly always servers will be connected by cables to the network, because the cable connections remain the fastest. Workstations which are stationary (desktops) are also usually connected by a cable to the network, although the cost of wireless adapters has dropped to the point that, when installing workstations in an existing facility with inadequate wiring, it can be easier and less expensive to use wireless for a desktop.

Wide Area Network

Wide Area Networks (WANs) connect networks in larger geographic areas, such as Florida, the United States, or the world. Dedicated transoceanic cabling or satellite uplinks may be used to connect this type of global network.

Using a WAN, schools in Florida can communicate with places like Tokyo in a matter of seconds, without paying enormous phone bills. Two users a half-world apart with workstations equipped with microphones and a webcams might teleconference in real time. A WAN is complicated. It uses multiplexers, bridges, and routers to connect local and metropolitan networks to global communications networks like the Internet. To users, however, a WAN will not appear to be much different than a LAN.

Example of an Advantages of Installing a School Network

User access control.

> Modern networks almost always have one or more servers which allows centralized management for users and for network resources to which they have access. User credentials on a privately-owned and operated network may be as simple as a user name and password, but with ever-increasing attention to computing security issues, these servers are critical to ensuring that sensitive information is only available to authorized users.

Information storing and sharing.

> Computers allow users to create and manipulate information. Information takes on a life of its own on a network. The network provides both a place to store the information and mechanisms to share that information with other network users.

Connections.

Administrators, instructors, and even
students and guests can be connected using
the campus network.

Services.

The school can provide services, such as
registration, school directories, course
schedules, access to research, and email
accounts, and many others. (Remember,
network services are generally provided by
servers).

Internet.

The school can provide network users with
access to the internet, via an internet
gateway.

Computing resources.

The school can provide access to special
purpose computing devices which individual
users would not normally own. For example,
a school network might have high-speed
high quality printers strategically located
around a campus for instructor or student
use.

Flexible Access.

School networks allow students to access their information from connected devices throughout the school. Students can begin an assignment in their classroom, save part of it on a public access area of the network, then go to the media center after school to finish their work. Students can also work cooperatively through the network.

Workgroup Computing.

Collaborative software allows many users to work on a document or project concurrently. For example, educators located at various schools within a county could simultaneously contribute their ideas about new curriculum standards to the same document, spreadsheets, or website.

Disadvantages of Installing a School Network

Expensive to Install.

Large campus networks can carry hefty price tags. Cabling, network cards, routers, bridges, firewalls, wireless access points, and software can get expensive, and the

29 | P a g e
Cisco
N e t w o r k s   F o r   B e g i n n e r s

installation would certainly require the
services of technicians. But, with the ease of
setup of home networks, a simple network
with internet access can be setup for a small
campus in an afternoon.

Requires Administrative Time.

Proper maintenance of a network requires
considerable time and expertise. Many
schools have installed a network, only to
find that they did not budget for the
necessary administrative support.

Servers Fail.

Although a network server is no more
susceptible to failure than any other
computer, when the files server "goes down"
the entire network may come to a halt.
Good network design practices say that
critical network services (provided by
servers) should be redundant on the network
whenever possible.

Cables May Break.

The Topology chapter presents information
about the various configurations of cables.
Some of the configurations are designed to
minimize the inconvenience of a broken

cable; with other configurations, one broken cable can stop the entire network.

Security and compliance.

Network security is expensive. It is also very important. A school network would possibly be subject to more stringent security requirements than a similarly-sized corporate network, because of its likelihood of storing personal and confidential information of network users, the danger of which can be compounded if any network users are minors. A great deal of attention must be paid to network services to ensure all network content is appropriate for the network community it serves.

How does a computer network work

Specialized devices such as switches, routers, and access points form the foundation of computer networks.

Switches connect and help to internally secure computers, printers, servers, and other devices to networks in homes or organizations. Access points are switches that connect devices to networks without the use of cables.

Routers connect networks to other networks and act as dispatchers. They analyze data to be sent across a network, choose the best routes for it, and send it on its way. Routers connect your home and business to the world and help protect information from outside security threats.

While switches and routers differ in several ways, one key difference is how they identify end devices. A Layer 2 switch uniquely identifies a device by its "burned-in" MAC address. A Layer 3 router uniquely identifies a device's network connection with a network-assigned IP address.

Today, most switches include some level of routing functionality.

MAC and IP addresses uniquely define devices and network connections, respectively, in a network. A MAC address is a number assigned to a network interface card (NIC) by a device's manufacturer. An IP address is a number assigned to a network connection.

How is computer networking evolving?

Modern-day networks deliver more than connectivity. Organizations are embarking on transforming themselves digitally. Their networks are critical to this transformation and to their success. The types of network architectures that are evolving to meet these needs are as follows:

- Software-defined (SDN): In response to new requirements in the "digital" age, network architecture is becoming more programmable, automated, and open. In software-defined networks, routing of traffic is controlled centrally through software-based mechanisms. This helps the network to react quickly to changing conditions.

- Intent-based: Building on SDN principles, intent-based networking (IBN) not only introduces agility but also sets up a network to achieve desired objectives by automating operations extensively, analyzing its performance, pinpointing problematic areas, providing all-around security, and integrating with business processes.

- Virtualized: The underlying physical network infrastructure can be partitioned logically, to create multiple "overlay" networks. Each of these logical networks can be tuned to meet specific security, quality-of-service (QoS), and other requirements.

- Controller-based: Network controllers are crucial to scaling and securing networks. Controllers automate networking functions by translating business intent to device configurations, and they monitor devices continuously to help ensure performance and security. Controllers simplify operations and help organizations respond to changing business requirements.

- Multidomain integrations: Larger enterprises may construct separate networks, also called networking domains, for their offices, WANs, and data centers. These networks communicate with one another through their controllers. Such cross-network, or multidomain, integrations generally involve exchanging relevant operating parameters to help ensure that desired business outcomes that span network domains are achieved.

Only Cisco offers a complete portfolio of modern network architectures for access, WANs, data centers, and cloud.

What is an IP Address – Definition and Explanation

IP address definition

An IP address is a unique address that identifies a device on the internet or a local network. IP stands for "Internet Protocol," which is the set of rules governing the format of data sent via the internet or local network.

In essence, IP addresses are the identifier that allows information to be sent between devices on a network: they contain location information and make devices accessible for communication. The internet needs a way to differentiate between different computers, routers, and websites. IP addresses provide a way of doing so and form an essential part of how the internet works.

What is an IP Address?

An IP address is a string of numbers separated by periods. IP addresses are expressed as a set of four numbers — an example address might be 192.158.1.38. Each number in the set can range from 0 to 255. So, the full IP addressing range goes from 0.0.0.0 to 255.255.255.255.

IP addresses are not random. They are mathematically produced and allocated by the Internet Assigned Numbers Authority (IANA), a division of the Internet Corporation for Assigned Names and Numbers (ICANN). ICANN is a non-profit organization that was established in the United States in 1998 to help maintain the security of the internet and allow it to be usable by all. Each time anyone registers a domain on the internet, they go through a domain name registrar, who pays a small fee to ICANN to register the domain.

Watch this video to learn what IP address is, why IP address is important and how to protect it from hackers:

How do IP addresses work

If you want to understand why a particular device is not connecting in the way you would expect or you want to troubleshoot why your network may not be working, it helps understand how IP addresses work.

Internet Protocol works the same way as any other language, by communicating using set guidelines to pass information. All devices find, send, and exchange information with other connected devices using this protocol. By speaking the same language, any computer in any location can talk to one another.

The use of IP addresses typically happens behind the scenes. The process works like this:

1. Your device indirectly connects to the internet by connecting at first to a network connected to the internet, which then grants your device access to the internet.

2. When you are ~~at~~ home, that network will probably be your Internet Service Provider (ISP). At work, it will be your company network.

3. Your IP address is assigned to your device by your ISP.

4. Your internet activity goes through the ISP, and they route it back to you, using your IP address. Since they are giving you access to the internet, it is their role to assign an IP address to your device.

5. However, your IP address can change. For example, turning your modem or router on or off can change it. Or you can contact your ISP, and they can change it for you.

6. When you are out and about — for example, traveling — and you take your device with you, your home IP address does not come with you. This is because you will be using another network (Wi-Fi at a hotel, airport, or coffee shop, etc.) to access the internet and will be using a different (and temporary) IP address, assigned to you by the ISP of the hotel, airport or coffee shop.

   As the process implies, there are different types of IP addresses, which we explore below.

Types of IP addresses

There are different categories of IP addresses, and within each category, different types.

Consumer IP addresses

Every individual or business with an internet service plan ~~will~~ have two types of IP addresses: their private IP addresses and their public IP address. The terms public and private relate to the network location — that is, a private IP address is used inside a network, while a public one is used outside a network.

Private IP addresses

Every device that connects to your internet network has a private IP address. This includes computers, smartphones, and tablets but also any Bluetooth-enabled devices like speakers, printers, or smart TVs. With the growing internet of things, the number of private IP addresses you have at home is probably growing. Your router needs a way to identify these items separately, and many items need a way to recognize each other. Therefore, your router generates private IP addresses that are unique identifiers for each device that differentiate them on the network. Public IP addresses

A public IP address is the primary address associated with your whole network. While each connected device has its own IP address, they are also included within the main IP address for your network. As described above, your public IP address is provided to your router by your ISP. Typically, ISPs have a large pool of IP addresses that they distribute to their customers. Your public IP address is the address that all the devices outside your internet network will use to recognize your network.

Public IP addresses

Public IP addresses come in two forms – dynamic and static.

Dynamic IP addresses

Dynamic IP addresses change automatically and regularly. ISPs buy a large pool of IP addresses and assign them automatically to their customers. Periodically, they re-assign them and put the older IP addresses back into the pool to be used for other customers. The rationale for this approach is to generate cost savings for the ISP. Automating the regular movement of IP addresses means they don't have to carry out specific actions to re-establish a customer's IP address if they move home, for example. There are security benefits, too, because a changing IP address makes it harder for criminals to hack into your network interface.

Static IP addresses

In contrast to dynamic IP addresses, static addresses remain consistent. Once the network assigns an IP address, it remains the same. Most individuals and businesses do not need a static IP address, but for businesses that plan to host their own server, it is crucial to have one. This is because a static IP address ensures that websites and email addresses tied to it will have a consistent IP address — vital if you want other devices to be able to find them consistently on the web.

This leads to the next point — which is the two types of website IP addresses.

There are two types of website IP addresses

For website owners who don't host their own server, and instead rely on a web hosting package — which is the case for most websites — there are two types of website IP addresses. These are shared and dedicated.

Shared IP addresses

Websites that rely on shared hosting plans from web hosting providers will typically be one of many websites hosted on the same server. This tends to be the case for individual websites or SME websites, where traffic volumes are manageable, and the sites themselves are limited in terms of the number of pages, etc. Websites hosted in this way will have shared IP addresses.

Dedicated IP addresses

Some web hosting plans have the option to purchase a dedicated IP address (or addresses). This can make obtaining an SSL certificate easier and allows you to run your own File Transfer Protocol (FTP) server. This makes it easier to share

42 | P a g e
Cisco
N e t w o r k s F o r B e g i n n e r s

and transfer files with multiple people within an organization and allow anonymous FTP sharing options. A dedicated IP address also allows you to access your website using the IP address alone rather than the domain name — useful if you want to build and test it before registering your domain.

How to look up IP addresses

The simplest way to check your router's public IP address is to search "What is my IP address?" on Google. Google will show you the answer at the top of the page.

Other websites will show you the same information: they can see your public IP address because, by visiting the site, your router has made a request and therefore revealed the information. The site IPLocation goes further by showing the name of your ISP and your city.

Generally, you will only receive an approximation of location using this technique — where the provider is, but not the actual device location. If you are doing this, remember to log out of your VPN too. Obtaining the actual physical location address for the public IP address usually requires a search warrant to be submitted to the ISP.

Finding your private IP address varies by platform:

In Windows:

- Use the command prompt.
- Search for "cmd" (without the quotes) using Windows search
- In the resulting pop-up box, type "ipconfig" (no quote marks) to find the information.

On a Mac:

- Go to System Preferences
- Select network — and the information should be visible.

On an iPhone:

- Go to Settings
- Select Wi-Fi and click the "i" in a circle () next to the network you are on — the IP address should be visible under the DHCP tab.

If you need to check the IP addresses of other devices on your network, go into the router. How you access the router depends on the brand and the software it uses. Generally, you should be able to type the router's gateway IP address into a web browser on the same network to access it. From there, you will need to navigate to something like "attached devices," which should display a list of all the devices currently or recently attached to the network — including their IP addresses.

Cisco Network devices

Router
 Switch
 Multilayer Switch
 Cisco ASA
 Database

 Cisco CallManager
 IP Phone
 Access Server
 VPN Concentrator
 PIX Firewall

 Router with Firewall
 ATM Switch
 CSU/DSU
 Web Server
 Server
 Hub

 Mac
 PC
 Laptop
 100BaseT Hub
 Repeater

 Bridge
 IP Telephony Router
 uBR910 Cable DSU
 Access Point
 Modem

 Host
 Printer
 Headquarters
 Branch Office

Home Office

Ethernet Connection

Serial Line Connection

Network Cloud

Router

 Switch

 Multilayer Switch

 Cisco ASA

 Database

 Cisco CallManager

 IP Phone

 Access Server

 VPN Concentrator

 PIX Firewall

 Router with Firewall

 ATM Switch

 CSU/DSU

 Web Server

 Server

 Hub

 Mac

 PC

 Laptop

 100BaseT Hub

 Repeater

 Bridge

 IP Telephony Router

  uBR910 Cable DSU

 Access Point

 Modem

 Host

 Printer

 Headquarters

 Branch Office

 Home Office

Ethernet Connection

Serial Line Connection

Network Cloud

Network devices

Let's take a look at the network devices commonly found in today's LANs..

Hubs

A **hub** serves as a central point to which all of the hosts in a network connect to. A Hub is an OSI Layer 1 device and has no concept of Ethernet frames or addressing. It simply receives a signal from one port and sends it out to all other ports. Here is an example 4-port Ethernet hub (source: Wikipedia):

Today, hubs are considered obsolete and switches are commonly used instead.

Switches

Like hubs, a switch is used to connect multiple hosts together, but it has many advantages over a hub. Switch is an OSI Layer 2 device, which means that it can inspect received traffic and make forwarding decisions. Each port on a switch is a separate collision domain and can run in a full duplex mode (photo credit: Wikipedia).

Routers

A router is a device that routes packets from one network to another. A router is most commonly an OSI Layer 3 device. Routers divide broadcast domains and have traffic filtering capabilities.

The picture below shows a typical home router:

What is a CISCO Packet Tracer?

The CISCO packet tracker was developed by the **CISCO** Company. It is a type of tool that provides the simulator to practice simple and complex networks. The main purpose of the CISCO pocket tracker is to help the student for the purpose of learning hand on experience in networking. It also provides specific skills for CISCO technology. This tool cannot replace the router or switch because this software has some inbuilt protocol. The interesting thing is that this device has not only the CISCO product but also it has some inbuilt networking support.

This tool also facilitates some technical concepts like CCENT and CCNA, where the packet utilizes all the technical concepts and networking systems.

This packet also helps the student to complete their assignment by working on their own or working with a team. It also helps the engineer to test their application before implementing them. Also, the engineers who work on network support can also deploy any changes also use the CISCO packet. First, the engineers test the changes they want to make. Then if all the changes worked perfectly, the packet proceeded toward deployment of the test.

With the help of this packet tracker, it is very easier for all the engineers to add or remove any simulated network devices. We can perform these operations in two steps. One is drag and drop user interface, and another is the command line interface.

Workspace for CISCO Packet Tracer

1. Logical

The logical workspace shows the logical network topology that is built by the user. It displays the connecting, placing, and clustering of virtual network devices.

2. Physical

In the physical workspace, we can see the physical implementation of the logical network. It also shows how the network devices such as switches, routers, and hosts are connected in a real network topology.

What is difference between simulator and emulator?

Simulation. A simulator creates an environment that mimics the behaviors, variables, and configurations that exist in an iOS app's production environment. An emulator is designed to mimic all of the hardware and software features for the Android app production environment of a real device.

Step 6: Install Cisco Packet Tracer

Once downloaded, you need to double click on packet tracer software to start the installation. You need to first go through the License Agreement and must accept the agreement terms to continue with the installation. So go ahead and check I accept the agreement checkbox and then Click Next.

In the next window, you need to provide the destination folder location where you want to install the Cisco Packet Tracer. By default, it will install under C:\Program Files folder location as shown below. Then click on Next.

Here you need to select the folder location to place the program's shortcut. You can choose different location as per your requirement. For now, we are going to use the default Cisco Packet Tracer folder as shown below. Then Click on Next.

If there is any additional task you would like to setup then choose your option below and click on Next.

If there is any additional task you would like to setup then choose your option below and click on Next.

Finally you will see the summary of all the setup tasks going to be performed as shown below. If everything looks fine then Click on Install.

The installation will start and the progress can be tracked on below screen.

Once the application is successfully installed, you will see below completing setup wizard with Launch Cisco Packet Tracer checkbox selected. If you would like to launch the packet tracer then leave the checkbox selected. Otherwise, uncheck it and then click on Finish.

Once the application is successfully installed, you will see below completing setup wizard with Launch Cisco Packet Tracer checkbox selected. If you would like to launch the packet tracer then leave the checkbox selected. Otherwise, uncheck it and then click on Finish.

Step 7 Launch Cisco Packet Tracer

Immediately after launching the packet tracer, you will see below dialog box asking to start the application in multi-user mode. You can choose the appropriate option as per your requirement. Here we would be running multi-user so we are clicking on Yes.

In the next step, you will be asked to Sign in using either Networking Academy account or Skills for All account to keep the application running. Since we have created account on Skills for All so we will click on this option to Sign in.

If you are already signed in, then probably it won't ask you to enter the user and password again, it will directly show you below successfully logged in to Cisco Packet Tracer message or else you need to provide your user name and password again which you have created in the earlier step.

You can close the above browser tab and simultaneously you will see below Cisco Packet Tracer application launched successfully. This confirms your installation and launching of application is now completed. You are ready to start your work.

First project

192.168.1.2/24   192.168.1.3/24

PC-PT   PC-PT
PC0   PC1

Double click on each PCO, and Go to Desktop, then IP

| PCO   — □ ✕ |

| Physical   Config   Desktop   Programming   Attributes |

IP Configuration   **X**

Interface   FastEthernet0

IP Configuration

○ DHCP   ⦿ Static

IPv4 Address   192.168.1.2

Subnet Mask   255.255.255.0

Default Gateway   0.0.0.0

DNS Server   0.0.0.0

IPv6 Configuration

○ Automatic   ⦿ Static

IPv6 Address   /

Link Local Address   FE80::260:47FF:FEE8:C890

Default Gateway

DNS Server

802.1X

☐ Use 802.1X Security

Authentication   MD5

Username

☐ Top

Double click on each PC1, and Go to Desktop, then IP

PC1 — □ ×

Physical   Config   Desktop   Programming   Attributes

IP Configuration [X]

Interface   FastEthernet0

IP Configuration

○ DHCP   ◉ Static

IPv4 Address   192.168.1.3

Subnet Mask   255.255.255.0

Default Gateway 0.0.0.0

DNS Server   0.0.0.0

IPv6 Configuration

○ Automatic   ◉ Static

IPv6 Address   / [ ]

Link Local Address   FE80::260:47FF:FE12:5D87

Default Gateway

DNS Server

802.1X

☐ Use 802.1X Security

Authentication   MD5

Username

☐ Top

Test the connectivity by using the command PING on PCO on your CMD

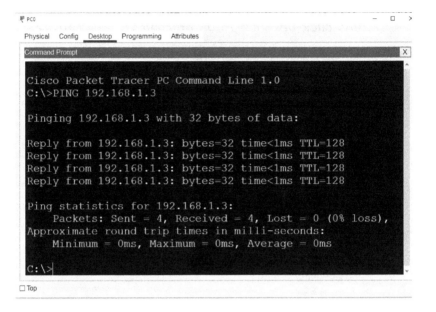

Project 2

Connect many computers using a switch

➢ Double click on each PC4, and Go to Desktop, then IP

➢ Do the same to each computer.

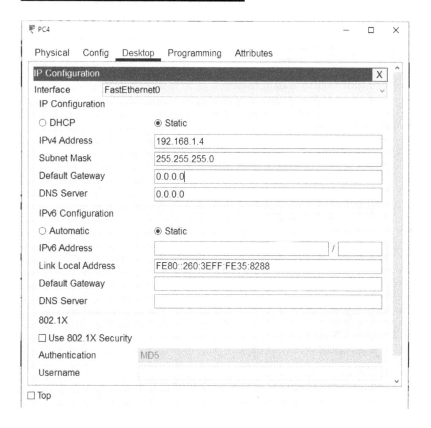

> ➢ Double click on each PC5, and Go to
>   Desktop, then IP

PC5   — ☐ ✕

Physical   Config   Desktop   Programming   Attributes

IP Configuration	X

Interface   FastEthernet0   ⌄

IP Configuration

○ DHCP   ◉ Static

IPv4 Address   192.168.1.5

Subnet Mask   255.255.255.0

Default Gateway   0.0.0.0|

DNS Server   0.0.0.0

IPv6 Configuration

○ Automatic   ◉ Static

IPv6 Address   /

Link Local Address   FE80::2D0:FFFF:FEE8:B58C

Default Gateway

DNS Server

802.1X

☐ Use 802.1X Security

Authentication   MD5

Username

☐ Top

Test connectivity

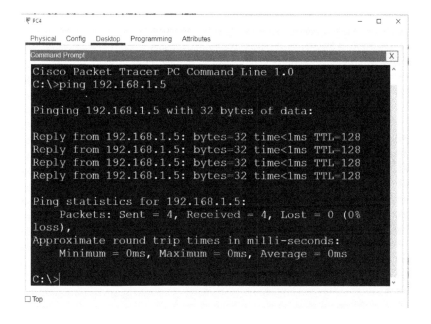

Getting Started with Cisco Switch Commands

Before we begin, get to know what hardware you're using, fire up your CLI and download PuTTY.

<u>PuTTy100% Free Download</u>

The first step is to check what hardware you're using before you begin. If you're using a Cisco switch you need to know what model you have.

You also want to check the physical state of the device and verify that none of the cables are damaged. You can turn the router on to make sure there is no damage to the lighting/indicators.

To discover the model of Cisco switches on your network using PuTTY, you'll need to establish a Secure Shell (SSH) or a Telnet connection to each switch individually.

Here are the steps:

1. **Launch PuTTY**: Open PuTTY, select the type of connection you want to make (SSH or Telnet), enter the switch's IP address, and then click 'Open'.

2. **Log in**: You will be prompted for your login credentials. Upon successful login, you will be placed at the command line prompt.

3. **Find the Model**: Type the following command to get the model information:

   show version

This command will display a range of data about the switch's software version, uptime, and hardware configuration, including the model number.

Configure a Cisco Switch with these 10 Steps	
Step 1	Connect the Switch to PuTTY
Step 2	Enter Privileged EXEC Mode and Set a Hostname for the Switch
Step 3	Assign a Password to the Switch
Step 4	Configure Telnet and Console Access Passwords
Step 5	Configure IP Addresses With Telnet Access
Step 6	Configure a Network Management IP address (or Management Interface)
Step 7	Assign a Default Gateway to the Switch
Step 8	Disable Unused Open Ports
Step 9	Save Your System Configuration Settings

Step 10	Configure NetFlow to Manage Your Cisco Switch (Optional)

Remember to repeat this process for each switch on your network.

Now that you've made sure the device is in working order you're ready to start configuring. In this guide, we're going to perform a **Cisco switch configuration** through the **command-line interface** (CLI) with the open-source SSH/Telnet client PuTTY (although you can use another tool if you prefer). If for any reason putty is not an option for your setup, you can get similar results with a PuTTY alternative.

1. Connect the Switch to PuTTY

To start configuration, you want to connect the switch console to PuTTY. You can do this by doing the following:

1. Connect the switch to PuTTY with a 9-pin serial cable.

2. Now open PuTTY and the PuTTY Configuration window will display. Go to the **Connection type** settings and check the **Serial** option (shown below).

3. Go to the **Category** list section on the left-hand side and select the **Serial** option.

4. When the options controlling local serial lines page displays enter the COM port your network is connected to in the **Serial line to connect to** box e.g. **COM1**.

5. Next, enter the digital transmission speed of your switch model. For 300 and 500 Series Managed Switches, this is **115200**.

6. Go to the **Data bits** field and enter **8**.

7. Now go to the **Stops bits** field and enter **1**.

8. Click on the **Parity** drop-down menu and select the **None** option.

9. Go to the **Flow Control** drop-down menu and select the **None** option.

Save Your Settings and Start the PuTTY CLI

To save your PuTTY settings for your next session do the following:

1. Click on the **Session** option from the **Category list** on the left-hand side of the

page.

2. Go to the **Saved Session** field and enter a name for your settings e.g. **Comparitech.**
3. Click the **Save** button to store the settings.
4. Press the **Open** button at the bottom of the page to launch the CLI.

The following message will display in the command prompt:

Switch>

2. Enter Privileged EXEC Mode and Set a Hostname for the Switch

Type in the enable command to enter privileged EXEC mode (you don't need a password at this stage because you're under the default configurations which don't have one!):

Enable

Next, enter Global Configuration Mode and enter the following command:

Switch# configure terminal
Switch(config)#

You can make the switch easier to locate in the network by assigning a hostname. Enter the following command to assign a hostname:

Switch(config)# hostname access-switch1
access-switch1(config)#1

3. Assign a Password to the Switch

Once you've assigned a hostname you will want to create a password to control who has access to the privileged EXEC mode (to prevent everyone from being able to log in). To assign an administrator password to enter the following command:

access-switch1(config)# enable secret COMPARI7ECH

Remember to pick a strong password so that it's harder to figure out.

4. Configure Telnet and Console Access Passwords

The next step is to configure passwords for Telnet and console access. Configuring passwords for these is important because it makes your switch more secure. If someone without authorization gains telnet access then it puts your network at serious risk. You can configure passwords by entering the following lines (See the top paragraph for Telnet and the bottom paragraph for Console access).

Telnet
access-switch1(config)# line vty 0 15

access-switch1(config-line)# password COMPARI7ECH

access-switch1(config-line)# login

access-switch1(config-line)# exit

access-switch1(config)#
Console
access-switch1(config)# line console 0

access-switch1(config-line)# password
COMPARI7ECH

access-switch1(config-line)# login

access-switch1(config-line)# exit

access-switch1(config)#

5. Configure IP Addresses With Telnet Access

The next step is to decide which IP addresses will
have access to Telnet, and add them with the
PuTTY CLI. To select permitted IP's enter the
following command (replace the listed IPs with the
IPs of the components you want to grant
permission to):

access-switch1(config)# ip access-list standard TELNET-ACCESS

access-switch1(config-std-nacl)# permit 216.174.200.21

access-switch1(config-std-nacl)# permit 216.174.200.21

access-switch1(config-std-nacl)# exit

You can also configure your network's access control lists (ACLs) to virtual terminal (VTY) lines. ACLs ensure that only the administrator can connect to the router through Telnet.

access-switch1(config)# line vty 0 15

access-switch1(config-line)# access-class TELNET-ACCESS in

access-switch1(config-line)# exit

access-switch1(config)#

6. Configure a Network Management IP address (or Management Interface)

Next, you need to configure a network management IP address. Switches don't come with an IP address by default, meaning that you can't connect to it with Telnet or SSH. To solve this problem you can select a virtual LAN(VLAN) on the switch and create a virtual interface with an IP address. You can do this by entering the following command:

access-switch1(config)# interface vlan 1

access-switch1(config-if)# ip address 10.1.1.200 255.255.255.0

access-switch1(config-if)# exit

access-switch1(config)#

The new IP management address is located in VLAN1, which other computers will now use to connect.

7. Assign a Default Gateway to the Switch

At this stage, you want to assign a default gateway to the switch. The default gateway is essentially the address of the router that the switch will be communicating with. If you don't configure a default gateway then VLAN1 will be unable to send traffic to another network. To assign the default gateway, enter the command below (change the IP address to that of your router).

access-switch1(config)# ip default-gateway 10.1.1.254

8. Disable Unused Open Ports

As a best practice, it is a good idea to disable any unused open ports on the switch. Cyber-criminals often use unsecured ports as a way to breach a network. Closing these ports down reduces the number of entry points into your network and makes your switch more secure. Enter the range of ports you want to close by entering the following command (you would change 0/25-48 to the ports that you want to close):

access-switch1(config)# interface range fe 0/25-48

access-switch1(config-if-range)# shutdown

access-switch1(config-if-range)# exit

access-switch1(config)#

9. Save Your System Configuration Settings

Once you've finished configuring the router it's time to save your system configuration. Saving the configuration will make sure that your settings are the same when you open up your next session. To save enter the following command:

access-switch1(config)# exit
access-switch1# wr

Always remember to save any changes to your settings before closing the CLI.

10. Configure NetFlow to Manage Your Cisco Switch (Optional)

It is also a good idea to use a network traffic analyzer to monitor network traffic. As a Cisco device, your switch will have the communication protocol NetFlow. However, it must be configured first. You can configure NetFlow by completing the four steps below. Before we begin, enter Global Configuration Mode by executing the following command:

Switch# configure terminal

Create a flow record

1. The first step is to create a flow record (you can change the name). You can do this by entering the following command:

   #flow record Comparitechrecord

2. After you've entered the previous command you need to set the IPv4 source address, IPv4 destination address, iPv4 protocol, transport source-port, transport destination-port, IPv4 dos, interface input, and interface output. You can do this by entering the following command:

3. **Switch# match ipv4 source address**

4.

5. Switch# match ipv4 destination address

6.

7. Switch# match ipv4 protocol

8.

9. Switch# match transport source-port

10.

11. Switch# match transport destination-port

12.

13. Switch# match ipv4 tos

14.

15. Switch# match interface input

16.

Switch# collect interface output

17. To finish configuring the flow record and define the type of data you're going to collect, enter the following switch configuration commands:

18. Switch# collect interface output

19.

20. Switch# collect counter bytes

21.

22. Switch# collect counter packets

23.

24. Switch# collect timestamp sys-uptime first

25.

Switch# collect timestamp sys-uptime last

Create the Flow Exporter

1. You must now create the flow exporter to store the information that you want to export to an external network analyzer. The first step is to name the flow exporter:

   Switch# flow exporter Comparitechexport

2. Enter the IP address of the server your network analyzer is on (Change the IP address):

   Switch# destination 117.156.45.241

3. Configure the interface that you want to export packets with:

   Switch# destination source gigabitEthernet 0/1

4. Configure the port that the software agent will use to listen for network packets:

Switch# transport UDP 2055

5. Set the type of protocol data that you're going to export by entering this command:

Switch# export-protocol netflow-v9

6. To make sure there are no gaps in when flow data is sent enter the following command:

Switch# template data timeout 60

Create a Flow Monitor

1. Once you've configured the flow exporter it is time to create the flow monitor. Create the flow monitor with the following command:<

Switch# flow monitor Comparitechmonitor

2. Associate the flow monitor with the flow record and exporter we configured earlier:

Switch# record Comparitechrecord

Switch# exporter Comparitechexport

3. To make sure that flow information is collected and normalized without a delay, enter the following command:

Switch# cache timeout active 60
Switch# cache timeout inactive 15

4. Enter the exit command:

Switch# exit

5. You need to input the interfaces that will collect the NetFlow data. If this is an ethernet interface you would enter the following:

Switch# interface gigabitEthernet 0/1

6. Use the following command to configure NetFlow on multiple interfaces (the input command will still collect data in both directions):

Switch# ip flow monitor Comparitechmonitor input

7. If you want to collect NetFlow data on only one interface then you must use the input and output command. So you would enter the following:

   Switch# ip flow monitor Comparitechmonitor input
   Switch# ip flow monitor Comparitechmonitor output

8. Exit configuration mode by entering the following command:

   Switch# exit

9. Save your settings to finish.

Configure a Cisco Switch for Peace of Mind!

Completing simple tasks like configuring passwords and creating network access lists controls who can access the switch can enable you to stay secure online. Incomplete or incorrect configurations are a vulnerability that attackers can exploit.

Configuring a Cisco switch is only half the battle, you also have to regularly monitor its status. Any performance issues with your switch can have a substantial impact on your users.

Using a network monitoring tool and network analyzer can help you to monitor switches remotely and review performance concerns. Taking the time out of your day to configure a switch and assign strong passwords gives you peace of mind so that you can communicate safely online.

Cisco Switch Configuration & Commands FAQs

How to configure a trunk port on a Cisco 2960 switch?

To configure a trunk port on a Cisco 2960 switch:

1. Enter configuration mode:

configure terminal

2. Specify the port to use:

interface <interface-id>

3. Configure the port as a Layer 2 trunk:

switchport mode {dynamic {auto | desirable} | trunk}

These options mean:

- **dynamic auto** – The Default. Creates a trunk link if the neighboring interface is set to trunk or desirable mode.
- **dynamic desirable** – Creates a trunk link if the neighboring interface is set to trunk, desirable, or auto mode.
- **trunk** – Sets the interface in permanent trunking mode.

4. Specify a default VLAN to use for back up. This is optional:

switchport access vlan <vlan-id>

5. Specify the native VLAN:

switchport trunk native vlan <vlan-id>

6. Exit the config mode:

end

How do I set a static IP on a Cisco switch?

A problem with the GUI interface of Cisco switches makes it impossible to assign a static IP address to an interface. Follow these steps for a workaround:

1. Create a text file on your PC. It doesn't matter where you save it or what you call it, but make sure you remember where it is. Substitute real values for the tokens shown in angle brackets (<>) below. The text in the file should be:

Config t
Interface <VLAN ID>
No ip address DHCP
Y
No ip address <old IP address>
IP address <new IP address> <subnet mask>
Exit
IP default-gateway <gateway IP address>

2. Access the admin menu of the switch for **Switch Management**.

3. In the menu, click on **Administration**, then **File Management**, and then select **File Operations**.

4. In the File Operations screen, set the following:

- Operation Type: Update File
- Destination File Type: Running Configuration

- Copy Method: HTTP/HTTPS
- File Name: (Browse to select the file you created on your PC).

5. Click on **Apply**.

Networking terms

Term	Definition
3G	Third generation of mobile telecommunications technology, typically offering higher data rates than earlier generations.
4G	Fourth generation of mobile telecommunications technology, typically offering even higher data rates than 3G.
5G	Fifth generation of mobile telecommunications technology, offering faster

	speeds and higher bandwidth than 4G.
Access Control List (ACL)	A set of rules that controls traffic in and out of a network or individual device.
Address	Unique identifier for a specific computer or device on a network.
Address Resolution Protocol (ARP)	Protocol for mapping an Internet Protocol address (IP address) to a physical machine address that is recognized in the local network.
Administrator	User with full control over a network or individual computer.
Address Resolution Protocol (ARP)	Protocol used to map an IP address to a physical address, such as a MAC address.

Advanced Encryption Standard (AES)	Symmetric key algorithm used to encrypt and decrypt data.
Amazon Web Services (AWS)	Comprehensive, evolving cloud computing platform provided by Amazon.
Apache	Popular open-source web server.
Application Programming Interface (API)	Specific method prescribed by a computer software program for requesting services from another software program.
Asynchronous Transfer Mode (ATM)	Cell-based switching technique for voice, video, and computer data.
Auto Scaling	Cloud computing feature that provides the ability to scale an application up or down

	automatically according to conditions set by the user.
Bandwidth	Amount of data that can be transferred over a given period of time.
Bit	Smallest unit of data in a computer.
Bridge	Device that connects two or more networks together.
Broadcast	Message sent to all devices on a network.
Client	Device or software application that requests services from a server.
Cloud	Network of remote servers hosted on the internet and used to store, manage, and process data.

Cloud Computing	Ability to access applications and data over the internet.
Cluster	Group of computers that work together to provide high availability.
Code	Set of instructions that a computer can understand.
Collision	Condition that occurs when two devices on a network attempt to transmit at the same time.
Compiler	Program that converts code into a form that a computer can execute.
Crossover Cable	Type of Ethernet cable used to connect two devices of the same type, such as two computers.

Data Center	Facility used to house networking equipment and other computer systems.
Data Encryption Standard (DES)	Standard for encrypting data that was developed by the U.S. National Institute of Standards and Technology (NIST).
Data Link Layer	Second layer of the OSI model, which is responsible for error-free transfer of data frames from one node to another.
Data Mining	Process of extracting patterns from large data sets.
Database	Collection of data that can be accessed by computers.
Database Server	Server that stores and manages data in a database.

Dedicated Line	Physical connection between two devices that is not shared with any other devices.
Denial of Service (DoS)	Attack that prevents legitimate users from accessing a network or individual device.
Developer	Programmer who writes code to create software applications.
Dial-up	Type of internet connection that uses a telephone line.
Domain Name System (DNS)	System that converts human-readable domain names into numerical IP addresses.
Dynamic Host Configuration Protocol (DHCP)	Protocol for automatically assigning IP addresses to devices on a network.

Encryption	Process of converting data into a form that cannot be read by unauthorized individuals.
Ethernet	Popular type of physical network that uses twisted pair or fiber optic cables to connect devices.
Extranet	Private network that uses the public internet to securely connect two or more locations.
File Transfer Protocol (FTP)	Protocol used to transfer files from one computer to another over a network.
Firewall	Device or software application that filters traffic between two networks or between a device and a network.

Firmware	Software that is stored in a computer's read-only memory (ROM).
Gateway	Device that connects two networks with different protocols or two devices with different interfaces.
Gigabit Ethernet	Ethernet standard with a data transfer rate of one gigabit per second.
Hub	Device that connects multiple network devices together.
Hypertext Transfer Protocol (HTTP)	Protocol used to transfer web pages and other files on the World Wide Web.
Hypertext Transfer Protocol	Secure version of HTTP that is used to transfer sensitive data, such as credit card numbers.

Secure (HTTPS)	
IGMP (Internet Group Management Protocol)	Protocol used to manage multicast group membership.
Infrastructure as a Service (IaaS)	Form of cloud computing that delivers computer infrastructure on an as-a-service basis.
Intrusion Detection System (IDS)	System that monitors network traffic for signs of malicious activity.
Input	Data or instructions that are entered into a computer.
JavaScript	Programming language that is used to create interactive web pages.

Jitter	Variation in delay between data packets sent across a network.
LAN (Local Area Network)	Network that is confined to a relatively small area.
Leased Line	Point-to-point link between two devices in which each device has a dedicated connection to the other.
Internet Protocol version 4 (IPv4)	Previous version of the Internet Protocol (IP), which is being replaced by IPv6.
Internet Protocol version 6 (IPv6)	Latest version of the Internet Protocol (IP), which is the protocol used to route data on the internet.
Internet Service Provider (ISP)	Company that provides access to the internet.

IP Address	Unique identifier for a device on a network.
Malware	Short for "malicious software," it is any software designed to harm a computer or its user.
Modem	Device that converts digital signals to analog signals and vice versa.
Multicast	Message sent to a group of devices on a network.
NAT (Network Address Translation)	Technique used to allow devices on a private network to communicate with devices on a public network.
Netmask	Value used to specify which portion of an IP address represents the network and which portion represents the host.

Network	Group of two or more devices that are connected.
Network Interface Card (NIC)	Device that connects a computer to a network.
Network as a Service (NaaS)	Form of cloud computing that delivers network infrastructure as a service.
Open system interconnection model (OSI model)	Framework for understanding how data is transmitted between two nodes on a network.
Packet	Unit of data that is sent over a network.
Peer-to-Peer Architecture	Network architecture in which each computer or process on the network can act as both a client and a server.

Platform as a Service (PaaS)	Form of cloud computing that delivers a computing platform and/or solution stack as a service.
Protocol	Set of rules that govern communication between devices on a network.
Router	Device that forwards packets between networks or between devices on the same network.
Secure Sockets Layer (SSL)	Protocol for securing data transfer over the internet.
Server	Device or software application that provides services to other devices or software applications.
Service Pack	Collection of updates and fixes for a software program.
Simple Mail Transfer	Protocol used to send email.

Protocol (SMTP)	
Software as a Service (SaaS)	Form of cloud computing that delivers software as a service.
Spyware	Type of malware that gathers information about a user without their knowledge.
Structured Query Language (SQL)	Standard language for accessing and manipulating databases.
Subnet	Portion of a network that is isolated from the rest of the network.
Switch	Device that connects multiple devices together on a network and forwards packets between them.

101 | P a g e
Cisco
N e t w o r k s   F o r   B e g i n n e r s

Transmission Control Protocol (TCP)	Protocol used to transfer data over a network.
Trojan Horse	Type of malware that masquerades as legitimate software in order to trick users into installing it.
Unicast	Message sent to a single destination on a network.
User Datagram Protocol (UDP)	Protocol used to transfer data over a network.
Virtual Private Network (VPN)	Technique used to create a secure connection between two or more devices over a public network.
Virtual Machine (VM)	Software program that emulates the hardware of a computer.

Voice over IP (VoIP)	Technique used to transmit voice traffic over a data network.
Wide Area Network (WAN)	Network that covers a large geographical area.
Wireless Access Point (WAP)	Device that connects wireless devices to a wired network.
Wired Equivalent Privacy (WEP)	Security protocol for wireless networks.
Wi-Fi Protected Access (WPA)	Security protocol for wireless networks. It's an improvement over WEP and is required for networks that use 802.11n.
Worm	Type of malware that replicates itself and spreads to other computers on a network.

Zero Configuration Networking	Set of technologies that automatically configures IP addresses and other network settings without user intervention.
Zombie	Computer that has been infected with a virus and can be controlled by a remote attacker.
Zone	Logical grouping of network resources. Zones can be used to segment a network for security or performance reasons.
Zone Transfer	Process of copying DNS zone information from one DNS server to another.